D1397151

2/11/11

40-8-04

QBI

MTU

SUPER STRUCTURES OF THE WORLD

THE WORLD'S LARGEST BUILDING

BLACKBIRCH®
PRESS

THOMSON
GALE

San Diego • Detroit • New York • San Francisco • Cleveland • New Haven, Conn. • Waterville, Maine • London • Munich

For more information, contact
The Gale Group, Inc.
27500 Drake Rd.
Farmington Hills, MI 48331-3535
Or you can visit our Internet site at http://www.gale.com

LIBRARY OF CONGRESS CATALOGING-IN-PUBLICATION DATA

World's largest building / Elaine Pascoe, book editor.
    p. cm. — (Super structures of the world)
Summary: Describes the enormous building north of Seattle, Washington, where Boeing passenger jets are manufactured.
Includes bibliographical references and index.
  ISBN 1-56711-871-2 (hardback : alk. paper) — ISBN 1-4103-0187-7 (pbk. : alk. paper)
  1. Hangars—Washington—Everett—Juvenile literature. 2. Boeing airplanes—Design and construction—Juvenile literature. 3. Everett (Wash.)—Buildings, structures, etc.—Juvenile literature. [1. Hangars—Washington—Everett. 2. Boeing airplanes—Design and construction. 3. Airplanes—Design and construction. 4. Everett (Wash.)—Buildings, structures, etc.] I. Pascoe, Elaine. II. Series.

TL730.3.W67 2004
387.7'362—dc21   2003009271

Printed in China
10 9 8 7 6 5 4 3 2 1

WORLD'S LARGEST BUILDING

Today a trip that used to be measured in days or weeks can be completed in the amount of time it takes for dinner and a movie. Modern passenger jets have made the world a smaller place. But as amazing as today's aircraft are, a structure that gives birth to them is even more impressive.

Above: The Boeing manufacturing plant is the world's largest building and a massive super structure used to build the largest commercial airplanes.

The Boeing manufacturing plant in Everett, Washington, spits out more big planes than any other plant in history. And it is one of the world's most amazing super structures. At one end, millions of parts enter the building. At the other, the largest commercial airplanes ever to take flight roll out, ready to circle the globe.

Designed to produce the original jumbo jet, the 747, and updated for continued construction of today's wide bodies, the 767 and the 777, this building thirty miles north of Seattle is awe inspiring. There is more room under the roof of the Boeing plant than any other building in the world—98 acres, or 6.6 million square feet. That's enough to put all of Disneyland inside, and still have 14 acres left over. You could fit 75 football fields under this roof, 910 pro basketball courts, or a suburban development of about 2,000 homes.

Above: The Disneyland theme park could fit inside the Boeing plant's 6.6 million square feet of space.

Left: Two thousand homes could fit in the space underneath the plant's roof.

Left: Inside the Boeing factory, workers have built thousands of 747, 767, and 777 jets that have flown an estimated 13 billion travelers to their destinations.

Right: The front doors of the plant are enormous—a whopping eighty feet high by fifty feet wide.

Even the front doors are built to an almost unimaginable scale—about eighty feet high by about fifty feet wide. Behind the doors, twenty-four hours a day, seven days a week, a highly choreographed process turns parts into planes. The people in this factory have built thousands of wide-body jets. It's estimated that Boeing commercial airplanes have carried 13 billion passengers a distance that is equal to about 265,000 round trips to the moon.

PARTS IN, PLANES OUT

The manufacturing process is roughly the same for all three types of jets. Parts come to the factory semi-assembled, and each piece is put together to form larger sections—wings, tail sections, fuselage. Then these sections are joined at a central location, and the aircraft starts to look like an aircraft. As the plane moves closer to the large hangar doors, more pieces are added until it rolls out the front a complete jet. All three lines are in production simultaneously.

"We're proud of how fast we can actually build a 747," says Boeing director of manufacturing Jack Jones. "From the time the very first part that comes into this factory, to the time we actually deliver the plane to an airline customer, it's approximately four months."

 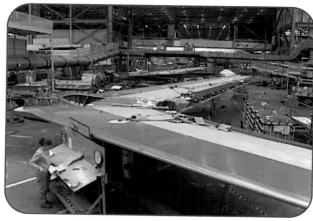

Above left: Workers at the plant complete the assembly of a 747 in about four months. Above right: The three commercial airliners are made of many pieced-together parts such as wings, tail sections, and fuselage.

Boeing's newest plane, the Triple Seven, comes together in just seventy days. Parts and some assemblies come from hundreds of vendors all over the world and all fifty of the U.S. states by rail, boat, air, and truck. Wing spars and skins are so big, they arrive on uniquely designed ultra-long trucks that actually require two drivers. Precision scheduling means the parts arrive as they're needed. The production schedule is as big and complex as the plant itself.

Right: Specially designed trucks transport the large airplane parts to the plant in Everett, Washington. The trucks are so big and long that they require two drivers to maneuver them.

Left: Boats, trains, planes, and trucks transport airplane parts to the Boeing plant from all over the world.

On the 777 wing line, the wings start taking shape with the help of automated riveting machines. The machines drill a hole between the frame and the skin, clean the hole, install the fastener, and shave the fastener head smooth. They do this task up to four times a minute. It would take four times longer if human hands were doing the work. And mere mortals can't duplicate the precision needed for the perfect wing surface. Smooth wing surfaces make for uninterrupted airflow and a more efficient airplane.

Top right: Special automated riveting machines help build the airplanes. Middle: These machines perfect the smoothness of the wing shape and work four times faster than human employees. Bottom: Airplanes require smooth wing surfaces for maximum efficiency.

The wing also holds fuel tanks, and every seam and every hole has to be sealed. To check for leaks, the wing is filled with ammonia gas. Then it's sprayed with a coating that'll turn blue if it comes in contact with any leaking gas.

The finished wings move to the wing-body join position, where they're attached to the body of the aircraft. This is a complicated and critical join. It's the strongest part of the Triple Seven, essentially taking all of the strain of lifting the 656,000-pound aircraft off the ground. Eventually, some of the stress gets spread through the entire fuselage. But if the wing assembly section is flawed in any way, this plane never gets off the ground. The wing-body assembly is the heaviest part of the Triple Seven. It requires two cranes to move this section, which weighs in excess of 100,000 pounds.

Above: Because the wing-body assembly is the heaviest part of the plane, operators use two cranes to move it.

Right: The wing allows for uninterrupted airflow and also contains the fuel tanks. The wing must be checked thoroughly for gas leaks.

BUILDING THE IMPOSSIBLE

Boeing's giant factory owes its existence to the 747, a jet that changed the face of flying. The largest passenger jet in existence, the 747 has flown 3.3 billion people—nearly half the world's population—since it first took to the skies.

747s are the largest passenger jets ever produced and have carried 3.3 billion people across the skies since their creation.

When Boeing first announced plans to build the jet, the company didn't even have a place to build it. In June 1966 the company announced that it had purchased the Everett site. But building the huge factory was a mighty risk for the Boeing company. And rumors were flying in the late 1960s that if the 747 project didn't take off, the company could be grounded permanently.

Every day Malcolm Stamper, the original manager for the 747 program, heard skeptics say he was working on an impossible project. "I got mail all the time, saying, 'Don't you know that this can't be done. You're not going to get off the ground,'" he recalls.

Malcolm Stamper
Retired Boeing Vice Chairman
Original 747 General Manager

Above: In the late 1960s, Malcolm Stamper, the original general manager of the 747 program, worked against many odds to build the biggest commercial jet in history. Below: The Boeing Corporation took a big risk when they built the Everett plant and the 747, but the company did not yet know the impact it would have on the world.

Before construction could get off the ground, the ground had to be leveled. Workers moved 8.5 million cubic yards of dirt from the site, more than twice the amount of earth moved to construct the Grand Coulee Dam. But no amount of grading could make up for the fact that the site was up on a plateau and three miles from the main railroad line. So the second steepest railroad spur in the United States was built to get plane parts from sea level up a 5.6 percent grade to the factory.

Above: Workers had to move 8.5 million cubic yards of dirt in order to level the ground before the construction crew could begin to build the plant.

Right: The crew moved more than twice the amount of dirt as was moved for construction of the Grand Coulee Dam (pictured).

With the building three-quarters finished, workers started loading the first airplane's parts in the back shops. It seemed an impossible task—the jet that could change the world or ruin a corporation was being built inside an incomplete plant that was breaking size records in its own right. The workers who took this challenge were a special breed.

They earned a nickname: the "Incredibles." Jack Jones, director of manufacturing for the Boeing 747-400, explains, "They were actually assembling the airplane as they were putting the roof on the end of the building. And they got this all done in unprecedented amount of time."

Above left: Workers earned themselves the moniker the "Incredibles" when they began to build the first 747 inside the plant that was still under construction.

Left: Boeing employees began assembly of the jet inside the plant before the roof was in place.

It wasn't all mud and deadlines. The big project spawned some fun too. To check the cleanliness of a pond that the construction created, fish were shipped in and dumped in the water. They survived, so from time to time workers would go out and catch a fish.

With the effort by the "Incredibles," everything was finished in September 1968. The first 747 emerged from its big new building to meet the world. And on a wet February day in 1969, the first 747, named the *City of Everett*, made aviation history. The plane that many said was too heavy to fly blasted into the sky.

Left: In February 1969 the first Boeing jet took to the sky and disproved all beliefs that the craft was too heavy to fly.

Right: Completed in September 1968, the first 747 was christened the City of Everett, *after its birthplace.*

Meanwhile, the construction of the mammoth plant changed the face of Everett forever. Before Boeing arrived, Everett was a small mill town. And while the paper mills were the economic backbone of the town, they also added an element that wasn't always appreciated.

"With the four pulp mills, Everett had its own unique odor," says local historian Larry O'Donnell. "People would come here visiting and kind of hold their noses."

When Everett got its jet plant, suddenly property values doubled and an influx of newcomers flooded the town. The new plant would employ twelve thousand to fifteen thousand people. Today, that number has almost doubled, and the big plant remains a big player in the town's economy and culture.

Top: The Boeing plant employs thirty thousand people and has greatly influenced the economy and culture of Everett.

Above left: The small mill town of Everett exploded with activity when the Boeing factory opened. As a result, both the town's population and its property values soared.

ON THE PRODUCTION LINE

Inside the giant plant, the process of building a jet remains the same. As the 777's wings are riveted together in one part of the plant, the tail section takes shape in another area.

Five and a half percent of the 777 is built of nonmetallic materials. The horizontal stabilizers in the tail section account for a lot of that amount. The stabilizers are 80 percent composite, a high-tech material that saves weight and thus adds to fuel efficiency. Lightweight materials helped the Triple Seven set a flight distance record of 12,455 miles without landing.

Left: The production process of the 777, or Triple Seven, is similar to those of the 747 and 767. However, the 777 is made of light-weight materials that helped it set a flight distance record of 12,455 miles.

This page: The wings of the colossal 777 are built in one section of the plant while the tail section is pieced together elsewhere.

The most recognizable piece of the plane, the fuselage, is actually built upside down and then turned right side up. With the two side-wall panels held upside down, 777 shift manager Rich Hendele explains, "We take the floor of the airplane and attach it from the top down. This helps our mechanics—they're constantly riveting down with the heavy rivet guns, rather than riveting up." Then the three-quarter section is lifted with an overhead crane and flipped over on a huge turning fixture, so the crown panel can be attached.

Rich Hendele
777 2nd Shift Factory Manager

Top: The fuselage is built upside down and later righted. This helps the mechanics attach the floor of the airplane.

Left: Shift manager Rich Hendele oversees production at the plant, specifically of the fuselage.

In the next few weeks, this empty shell will morph into a technological marvel. Insulation blankets, air conditioning ducts, ladders and rails to hold stow bins in place, and 150 miles of wiring go in every plane. Wire is one of the few parts made at the plant, in the largest wire-making facility in the world.

A process called "final body join" marks the point where parts finally become a jet. This step takes place during the nightshift, so fewer workers will be in harm's way as powerful cranes lift each of the assembled sections and place them in line to be joined. First, the wing and middle of the plane are flown into position. Next, the fore and aft sections of the plane float in. In two hours or so, the plane is temporarily pinned together, making a recognizable jumbo jet.

Right: The Boeing plant contains the largest wire-making facility in the world. Each plane needs 150 miles of wiring to run it.

A system of computer-guided lasers aligns the sections. Lasers home in on targets placed in each section, producing a perfectly straight airplane each and every time. From the nose to the tail of the plane, the difference in actual dimensions from the computer design is less than the width of a coin. Along with light-weight materials and a twin-engine design, the 777's slick airframe contributes to its incredible fuel economy.

No jumbos would be able to leave this factory at all if it weren't for the plant's highway in the sky—a thirty-one-mile network of eighteen cranes ninety feet above the factory floor. These cranes are capable of lifting up to forty tons. And still, to lift plane parts like the Triple Seven wing-body assembly, they need to double up.

Above: Eighteen cranes work together to lift planes and plane parts into the air. The crane network covers thirty-one miles of space in the Boeing plant.

Left: Computer-guided lasers help to keep the airplanes straight and to strictly follow the computer's original design.

A control tower is the command center for the aerial traffic within the factory. Crane operators must have no fear of heights and maintain a calm demeanor while dangling $8 million jet parts from their hooks, following signals from controllers. The crane ops work about half of their shift in a cab and the rest of the shift down below giving signals or doing other support jobs. They also alternate between three production lines, which helps keep the boredom level to a minimum.

Above: Crane operators work high up in the air and shift expensive jet parts through the air. Some parts cost as much as $8 million each.

Right: Crane operators also work on the ground to direct signals and support the three plane production lines.

This page: Once a jet is completed, it no longer has to rely on cranes and other machines. Instead, the jet rolls through the final steps of assembly on its own wheels.

A new jet rolls through the final assembly steps on its own wheels. Engines are installed. With the power on for the first time, the plane is tested from nose to tail—hydraulics, pneumatics, flaps, landing gear, autopilot systems, even the lavatories are put through their paces. Part of this

testing involves "flying" the jet without leaving the ground. An automated system simulates flight conditions to the plane's avionics, electronics, and mechanics.

The Triple Sevens, 767s, and 747s the plant churns out are all feats of aviation engineering. But the unsung hero in this saga is the building that provides protection for these projects under its ninety-eight-acre roof.

Top right: Workers turn on the power and test each plane to ensure that all its functions work properly.

Above: An automated simulation system "flies" the planes to check its avionics, electronics, and mechanics.

GETTING BIGGER

The first Boeing manufacturing plant was a small shop started by Bill Boeing in 1916. Military contracts through World War I and World War II were the backbone for Boeing's growth. Innovation kept the company flying. Its B-47 and B-52 bombers were the first swept wing jets. From those jets, the 707 and passenger jet service were born. Air travel exploded in the 1960s, and that growth led to the development of the 747 and its birthplace.

Left: In 1916 Bill Boeing started his company. His small manufacturing shop grew with the financial backing of military contracts.

Right: The company built bombers during World War I and World War II.

This behemoth building is packed from top to bottom with surprises. For one thing, you can go almost forever without seeing a supporting column. Too many big parts moving in too many different directions required the

engineers to create 300- to 350-foot clear spans. To hold up the massive roof over these gaping chasms, they used tremendous trusses of high-strength steel, put together on the ground and then raised into position with two large cranes.

Above: There are almost no visible supportive columns in the large warehouses of the Boeing plant.

Left: Instead of columns, high-strength steel trusses support the immense roof.

With ninety-eight acres of flat roof, a simple snowfall could have dire consequences. Snow is whisked off the roof as quickly as possible. Holding ponds control the runoff from rainstorms. The biggest one, dubbed Lake Boeing, holds enough water to float a cruise ship.

The building has grown with the demands placed on it. The original plant was expanded in 1980 to accommodate the 767, a wide-body jet that's smaller than the 747. The building underwent another major expansion again in 1993 for the 777 assembly line. The Triple Seven is a cutting edge, digital jet, the first Boeing has designed on computer instead of on paper.

Above left: Large ponds, like Lake Boeing itself, hold the runoff from rainstorms.

Left: The original building has undergone two expansions, once to accommodate the production of 767s and again for 777 assembly.

Today, looking at the factory from west to east gives you a visual history of its expansion. The original building, where 747s are still built, is the westernmost part of the plant. The 767s are built in the middle. And the newest part, the home of the Triple Seven, is the easternmost section.

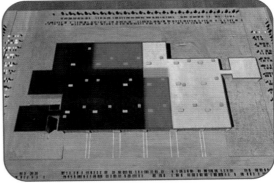

Boeing employees assemble the 747 jets in the western part of the building, the original building; the 767s in the middle section; and the Triple Sevens in the eastern area.

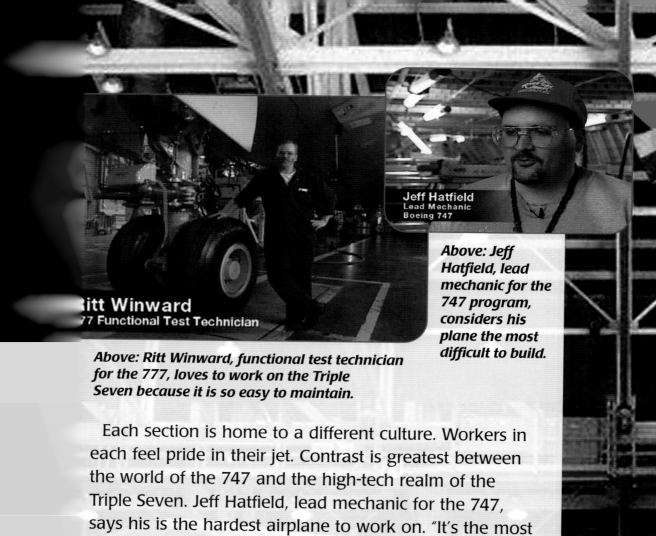

Jeff Hatfield
Lead Mechanic
Boeing 747

Ritt Winward
777 Functional Test Technician

Above: Jeff Hatfield, lead mechanic for the 747 program, considers his plane the most difficult to build.

Above: Ritt Winward, functional test technician for the 777, loves to work on the Triple Seven because it is so easy to maintain.

Each section is home to a different culture. Workers in each feel pride in their jet. Contrast is greatest between the world of the 747 and the high-tech realm of the Triple Seven. Jeff Hatfield, lead mechanic for the 747, says his is the hardest airplane to work on. "It's the most complicated. If you work here, you can almost work on any of the jetliners anywhere in Boeing," he says. But to electrician Ritt Winward, a 777 test technician, the Triple Seven's design and ease of maintenance make it "the neatest thing since sliced bread."

This spread: Each section of the massive building is home to a different creation and a different family of employees.

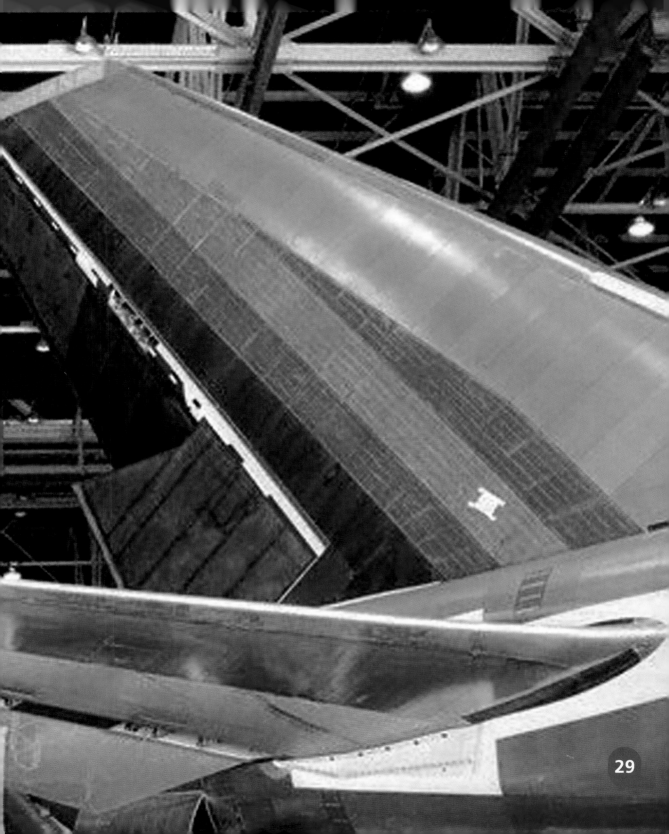

29

A CITY IN A BUILDING

When this factory is operating at top capacity, it's designed to churn out a stunning twenty-one airplanes per month, seven of each model. Though it's never reached that number, it has gotten close.

The plant employs thirty thousand workers, just four thousand fewer than the entire population of Washington's capital city, Olympia. Services include everything needed to run a small city. There's even a fire department—the largest private fire department in the world.

Top: The Boeing plant's design allows it to produce twenty-one jets each month when operating in optimal conditions. Although the plant has not yet achieved that goal, it still strives to meet it. Left: The plant is large enough to have its own fire department, the largest private fire department in the world.

Security is of paramount importance. Guard shacks, security badges, strict protocols, and a large staff make sure nothing untoward gets onboard the multimillion-dollar jets.

The plant's food service feeds about fourteen thousand workers a day. That calls for five hundred pizzas and a couple thousand sandwiches a day, and five hundred cases of pop and nine hundred pounds of coffee a week.

Top: The Boeing plant is like a small city. Its food service feeds fourteen thousand of the plant's thirty thousand employees each day.

Right: The kitchens bake five hundred pizzas a day.

The next generation of jet builders can be found at this plant as well. An on-site day care operates twelve hours a day, five days a week. Fifty teachers watch over two hundred kids. There's no need to tell you what the toy of choice is.

Most factories don't need their own highway system, but the Boeing plant has so many interior roads that traffic signs are a necessity and a map would be helpful. Bicycles are an important mode of transport within the plant. About seven thousand two- and three-wheelers keep the population moving. Lifts, jitneys and lightweight pickups ply the gridlike streets of the plant as well. So far, there has been no need for traffic cops.

Above: Seven thousand bicyclists ride through the "streets" inside the Boeing plant. The factory even has its own traffic signs.

Right: An on-site day care center looks after two hundred children while their parents work at the plant.

This factory's vast circumference provides a perk for folks who enjoy a good workout on their lunch break. One lap is two and a half miles.

No super structure is complete without secret passages. At Boeing's Everett plant, there's an underground tunnel system so vast that it even houses an auditorium. The tunnels allow people to move from one part of the factory to another without disrupting the work on the production floor.

Right: Many employees exercise simply by walking the 2.5-mile circumference of the building.

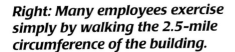

Left: An underground tunnel system below the plant permits people to cross through the plant with no disruption to production.

Left: In the summer, twelve hundred tourists visit the Boeing plant each day. The building is one of the top tourist attractions in Washington State.

Right: The plant's biggest expense is electricity. The 2001 energy bill was $22 million.

Opposite page: Boeing spends millions of dollars each year on electricity bills just to power the enormous plant.

The cost of powering this plant can be summed up in one word: Ouch! In 2001 the energy bill was $22 million. Most of that went for electricity.

The huge factory has even given rise to a subindustry that Boeing didn't plan for—tours. The plant has become one of Washington State's top tourist attractions, with twelve hundred people a day visiting during summer months.

It's hard to believe that anything coming out of Boeing's Everett plant can be bigger or more legendary than the jets it produces, but this place has spawned some tall tales. Some are urban myths, and some fall into the "truth is stranger than fiction" category.

Top: Presentations given in an on-site theater help people understand the production process.

Right: Street signs direct traffic throughout the massive factory.

Left: Myths and legends about the plant have circulated over the years.

There's a rumor that the building is so big it produces its own weather patterns inside. Not true. But here's a true tale: This building once helped bust a crook who bit off more hideout than he could chew. A bank robber, with police in hot pursuit, jumped the Boeing fence and ducked into the factory building. But the plant's vastness befuddled the bandit, and police found him quickly.

This criminal didn't just rob a bank. He robbed Boeing of millions by causing a brief pause in production. The cardinal rule in this plant can be summed up in two words: Don't stop. The building houses constant motion—parts in, jets out—twenty-four hours a day, seven days a week.

Above: Security guards may check ID cards now, but they once helped capture an on-the-run bank robber who chose the plant as his hideout.

Left: Production is constant in the Boeing plant. Jets are built twenty-four hours a day, seven days a week.

FINAL STEPS

Approximately every three nights, a brand new jet emerges into the night air for the very first time. At this point, the aircraft is essentially

completed. The interior fittings are in, and systems are all hooked up. Final touches and testing will cement a new jet's character before it leaves home for good.

Above left: A newly completed jet emerges from the plant every three nights.

Left: The jet will ultimately leave the plant after tests and last-minute touch-ups.

Top right: Assembled jets must cross a highway overpass to reach the paint hangar. To avoid stopping traffic, the jets leave the plant late at night.

Below left: The paint hangar is where workers hand wash the outer parts of the plane and paint on layers of coating.

Below right: A plane stays in the paint hangar for four days. There, workers clean its surface area and add six hundred pounds of paint.

The paint hangar, south of the plant, is where new jets get their personality. New jets typically are rolled out in the dead of night, so they won't stop traffic as they lumber across a highway overpass on the way to the paint hangar. Here the protective green vinyl coating is washed off. Then bare aluminum is hand cleaned, hand abraded, and coated with an anticorrosive substance. Only then can primer and topcoat go on. A 747 has twenty five hundred square feet of surface area and gains six hundred pounds in paint. The entire process typically takes four days.

The paint job isn't just cosmetic. A jet can take off in dry 95-degree weather, cruise for 14 hours at an altitude where the temperature can reach 60 degrees below zero, and then land in a place with 90-percent humidity. An unpainted aircraft would corrode with repeated exposure to those conditions.

Above: Several layers of anticorrosive substance, primer, and topcoat are painted onto the jet's surface areas.

Below: Jets need the many layers painted on in this hangar because they must be able to fly through harsh weather conditions without suffering corrosion.

Above: The protective green vinyl coating is first removed at the paint hangar.

The paint is approved and inspected by the Federal Aviation Administration. And it's not just slapped on with a brush and roller. Some decorative details, like the plum blossom on the tail of a China Airlines jet, are applied freehand. Not many painters get to work on a six-story canvas or have such a global audience.

Freshly painted, the jet awaits first flights, customer tests, and the flurry of paperwork, phone calls, and handshakes that precede final delivery. A Boeing wide-body jet can cost up to $230 million. Customers go over these machines thoroughly to make sure they're getting their money's worth.

Above: China Airlines employees hand paint the flowers that adorn their jets.

Below: Boeing jets can cost as much as $230 million. Boeing and its customers fill out a lot of paperwork before a jet's final delivery.

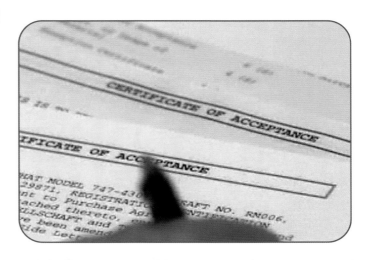

LOOKING AHEAD

Boeing has moved its corporate headquarters from Seattle to Chicago. That and a downturn in the airline industry have some people speculating about the future of this company's big-building, big-jets approach.

The company is making changes at the plant, mostly to create a leaner, cleaner production schedule. The 747 program recently began using a moving production line to help speed up the process. Jets will creep along at a rate of a foot per hour until they roll out the door. The goal is to knock about twenty days off the current production schedule, a 25 percent increase in efficiency.

Boeing aims to streamline its current production schedule and to reduce production time by up to twenty days.

This page: As part of its efforts to speed up assembly and revamp its production schedule, Boeing has started to use a moving production line in the 747 program.

Right: Boeing employees anticipate the building of a sonic cruiser like the one depicted here.

Left: This image shows what the sonic cruiser would look like if Boeing decided to expand its company and create the new aircraft.

There may be another jet in this plant's future—a fast one. Workers in the plant are hopeful that Boeing will manufacture a new sonic cruiser within the walls of their building. An expansion along the lines of what was done for the 767 and the Triple Seven is unlikely. But there is still plenty of room to grow.

This super structure has delivered for decades. Every jet that flies away from this plant is powerful proof of a job well done. Few products cement a worker's pride as completely as a brand new jet screaming down a runway and lifting itself skyward. Says 777 shift manager Rich Hendele, "When I see one flying through the air or when I go to the airport, I can point at that and say, 'I had a hand in that.' And I think just about everybody in this factory feels the same way. We take a lot of pride in what we do here."

Above: Boeing planes are symbols of the powerful plant that built them. Right: The Boeing plant and its jets have surpassed all expectations and still invoke pride in the people who work there.

 A factory that boggles our imaginations with its size also captivates us with what it creates. It's ironic, really. The biggest building in the world turns out the biggest commercial airliner in the world—and the world becomes a smaller place because of it.

Boeing jets are super flying structures built in the most massive super structure in the world.

GLOSSARY

aft the back part of a ship or airplane

aviation airplane operation, design, development, or manufacture

avionics electronics designed for use in aircraft

circumference the length of the external boundary of an object

choreograph to arrange or direct an activity

fore the front part of a ship or airplane

fuselage the central body of an aircraft, which contains crew, passengers, and cargo

hydraulics mechanical parts whose function involves liquids such as oil or water

jitney a small bus

pneumatics mechanical parts whose function involves air or other gases

truss an assembly of beams that make a rigid framework

wing skin the front wing surface on an airplane

wing spar a long, load-carrying beam in an airplane wing

INDEX

Boeing, Bill, 24
Boeing manufacturing plant, 3-5
    construction of, 12-15, 26
    cost of energy for, 35
    production capacity and, 30
    sections of, 27, 29
    747 program and, 10, 11, 13
    size of, 4, 23, 26, 33, 46
    tales about, 36-37
    tours of, 35
    traffic within, 32
    workers of, 29, 30, 31, 44
    See also services

Construction workers, 12-14
    see also Incredibles the
Control tower, 21
    crane operators and, 21
Corporate headquarters, Boeing, 42
Cranes, 19, 20, 25
    jumbo jet and, 20

Day care, 32

Everett, Washington, 3
    effect of plant on, 15, 33, 36

Federal Aviation Administration, 41
Final body join, 19
Fuselage, 6, 9, 18-19

Hendele, Rich, 18, 45
Hydraulics, 23

Incredibles, the, 13, 14

Jets
    cost of, 41
    747, 4, 6, 10-11, 13-14, 23, 26, 27,
        29, 39, 42
    767, 4, 23, 26, 27, 44
    777, 4, 7-9, 16, 18, 20, 23, 26, 27,
        29, 44, 45
Jones, Jack, 6, 13
Jumbo jet, 4, 19, 20

Lake Boeing, 26
Lasers, 20

Mechanic, 29

Paint hangar, 39-40
Production schedule, 37, 42
    night shift and, 19, 39
    precision scheduling and, 7
    speed of building and, 6, 38

Secret passages, 33
Services
    day care, 32
    fire department, 30
    food, 31
    security, 31
Stamper, Malcolm, 11

Triple Seven. *See* Boeing, the 777
Trusses, 25
Tunnel system, 33

Weather, protection from, 26
Wide-body jets, 4, 6, 41